THE HELLO MORNINGS CORE COMPONENTS
God. Plan. Move.
A TOPICAL BIBLE STUDY

Authors

Ali Shaw • Cheli Sigler • Karen Bozeman

Kat Lee • Lindsey Bell • Sabrina Gogerty

Hellomornings.org

TABLE OF CONTENTS

THE NEW Hellomornings BIBLE STUDY METHOD

We (The HelloMornings Team) are SO excited to share this new Bible study method with you!

The heart behind the method is "For Every Woman in Every Season." Whether you have 5 minutes or 50 minutes every morning, the HelloMornings study method can adapt to your schedule. We designed it so that a new believer won't feel overwhelmed and a seasoned Bible study student can dive deep into each passage.

We had three main goals in creating this method:

1. TO BUILD YOUR HABIT

Because building a daily God time habit is at the core of HelloMornings, we want to make sure you never feel overwhelmed with each day's study. If you only have 5 minutes, you can read the passage, write the verse and respond in a written prayer. If you have more time, you can dig deeper with one, two or all of the study "action steps." And if you want to go even deeper (or stretch the study out to a Saturday or Sunday) we are including group of study ideas in the front of the ebook so you'll always have a treasure trove of options to choose from.

2. TO BUILD YOUR GROUP

Our second goal was to create a method that encourages group interaction. Groups are integral to what we do here at HelloMornings. They are a way to build community, stay accountable to growth and learn from different perspectives.

But it's hard to find a group where everyone is at the same level of studying Scripture. That means with most Bible studies, some group members feel overwhelmed while others feel bored. Our goal is to bridge that gap and create content that not only fits any schedule, but also fits any level of study.

The beauty of this is that someone in your group who is brand new to the faith can daily dive into the same scriptures as a group leader who has been studying for decades. And the way we have formatted the content allows for each to learn and share in whatever way God is leading them so everyone can feel they have something to contribute, if they choose.

3. TO BUILD YOUR ROUTINE

In order to be the "hands and feet of Jesus," we need to:

1. Know Him—(God)
2. Understand His purpose for our lives—(Plan)
3. Follow His leading—(Move)

These are the core habits of HelloMornings.

God. Plan. Move.

Time with God is essential. And we believe that God has a purpose for each one of our lives. We also believe that He even has a purpose for each of our days. There are people He may want you to encourage today or ways He wants you to take action.

That is why we Plan. We want our daily planning to be done with His purposes in mind. Each daily worksheet has space for just a few of the most important tasks. Prayerfully planning is more powerful than any fancy productivity system because only God knows our heart, our purpose and our circumstances.

Finally, it's time to Move. This doesn't need to be a 3-mile run or a 25-minute workout. We simply want to be "fit for our calling"—i.e. have the energy to walk out the plan toward our purpose. If God has things He'd like us to do today, it's our responsibility to have the energy to do them. He does not give us more than we can handle.

For some, this might be simply drinking a morning glass of water. For others, it might be a short workout and for others it might be a healthy breakfast. The goal is just to do what we can to have the energy to respond to whatever God is calling us to each day. Kind of like an athlete makes sure to eat a good breakfast before a game so she has the energy to play well.

God. Plan. Move.

It doesn't need to take a long time. It could be as simple as a 5-minute routine of reading the daily passage, jotting down a few tasks and drinking a glass of water. Or it could be longer and more customized to your life.

Ultimately, we just want to start each day with the One who gave us all our days. And we want to plan our lives with the One who gives us our lives. And we want to Move wherever He may lead.

To a life well lived for the good of others and the glory of God,

The HelloMornings Team

SHARE THE STUDY

Will you consider helping us spread the word?

If you're in a HelloMornings group, invite all your group members to upgrade from the basic reading plan to this full study. It is well worth the price of a latte to study scripture deeply for 6 weeks and build a solid morning routine.

If you don't have a HelloMornings group, gather some friends together, send them to *HelloMornings.org/shop* to grab a copy of the study and spend the next 6 weeks journeying together! It's so much more fun and impactful when we learn and grow in community.

WAYS TO HELP OTHERS:

Use the hashtag *#HelloMornings* on Twitter or Instagram.

Share what you're learning on Facebook and link to *HelloMornings.org*

Tell your friends! Text, email or invite them to join you the next time you see them.

GET ALL THE RESOURCES:

We want to equip you to build a brilliant, God centered morning routine that leaves you feeling refueled and ready for action each day.

If you're not already on our email list, visit *HelloMornings.org* to download our free resources and receive our inspiring and idea-filled newsletter.

THE BIG BIBLE STUDY IDEA LIST

Each day of a HelloMornings study is filled with passages to read, a verse to write and plenty of action steps to take. But if you're ready to dive even deeper or you want to stretch our 5 day a week studies into 7 days, this list is the perfect way for you to add "tools" to your Bible study tool belt.

If you finish the study for the day and have more time, simply refer back to this "Big Bible Study Idea List" to select a few ways to dive even deeper into the passage you've been reading.

The best thing about this list is that it can be used on ANY section of scripture. So, if you want to do a study on 1 Corinthians 13 or look up all the verses on Faith, just use this list to build your own Bible study!

We want to equip you to study the Bible deeply regardless of whether you have a Bible study guide you're going through at the time or not. Try out each of these "tools" and add them to your Bible study "tool belt!"

READ AND WRITE

Ways to study scripture and dig deep into one passage.

READ

Simply read the passage. You can read it in your head, read out loud, read thoughtfully and slow, read in another translation.

WRITE

Honestly, this is my favorite way to start each morning. I *love* writing out scripture. There's something about the process of handwriting that both wakes me up and allows me to really marinate in the passage. It's also incredibly meaningful to have notebooks filled with handwritten scripture.

IDENTIFY KEY VERSES

In the passage you're reading, which verse holds the nugget of wisdom. Which verses explain the transformation of the main characters. Which verses speak most deeply to you in the season you're in right now?

HIGHLIGHT, UNDERLINE, BRACKET, CIRCLE, JOT

In this digital age, there is something therapeutic about words on a paper page and a pack of highlighters or colored pencils. I always loved looking at my grandmothers Bible filled with highlights, underlines, notes and circles.

Take time to circle commands, underline truths or highlight key verses in your favorite shade of pink. Bible study can be fun and colorful!

OBSERVE

Let your inner Nancy Drew loose. Uncover the 5 W's of the passage. Who, What, When, Where, Why and (don't forget) How. It's amazing how much we can learn from just naming the different elements of a passage or story.

ILLUSTRATE

In the margins of your Bible, or on a HelloMornings worksheet, get creative! Design word art focusing on a key point. Sketch the setting, characters or theme.

OUTLINE

Feeling more cerebral than creative? Outline the story or teaching. Highlight the main points and the sub-points to develop a greater understanding of where the author was coming from and what he was trying to communicate.

PERSONAL PARAPHRASE

Sometimes we learn best by teaching. Imagine you had to share the heart of the passage with a group of friends or a class of children, how would you paraphrase it? Or paraphrase it by incorporating your story into it and the things God has done in your life. You could even paraphrase it by simply incorporating your name in everywhere it has a generic pronoun.

QUESTIONS

Got questions? Just write them down. You can answer them later. Don't let your questions keep you from getting through the passage. Imagine you could interview the author, what would you ask?

RESPOND

A great way to dig deeper into scripture is to as a few simple questions. You can think about the answers as you read or you can write down your responses on the HelloMornings worksheet or in your own journal.

The Bible truly comes alive when we consider and pray about how God wants us to apply it to our own lives.

QUESTIONS TO CONSIDER:
- What does this say about God?
- What does this say about the church?
- What does this say about me?
- What truths are in this passage?
- Does this passage lead me to confess anything in prayer?
- What should I pray?
- What actions should I take?

- How can today be different because of this passage?
- What are some journaling questions?
- What is the lesson from this passage?
- Which key verse should I memorize this week?

RESEARCH

There is so much to be learned on every page of scripture. But sometimes we can take our study to a new level when we start flipping the pages and learning the "story behind the story."

Here are a few things you can research about the passage you are studying.

AUTHOR

Who wrote this passage? What do we know about him and how he fits into the story of the Bible? What were his circumstances? Why did he write it? Who was he writing to? Where was he when he wrote it? What had God done in his life to compel him to write this passage?

BACKGROUND

What was the background of the passage? What story or theme was introduced in previous verses or chapters of the book?

AUDIENCE

Who was the audience that the author was writing to? Why was it written to them? How do you think they responded to it? How would you have responded?

CONTEXT: CULTURAL, HISTORICAL, GRAMMATICAL

What was happening in history at the time the passage was written? What was the culture in which it was written like? How did the culture or the historical circumstances influence the author? Are there any grammatical rhythms or clues identifying or strengthening the authors meaning or ultimate intent?

CROSS REFERENCE

If you have a Bible with cross references (or using an online resource), look up all the verses associated with the passage. What can you learn from them and how do they influence the text?

COMMENTARIES

Read the commentary in your Bible, commentary books or at a trusted online source to gain even more insight into the passage.

TRANSLATIONS

Read the passage in multiple translations. How do they differ? How are they the same? What new truths can you glean from the variety of perspectives?

MAPS

Are there any maps in your Bible or online related to the passage you're studying? Follow the journey of the main characters. Look up modern day pictures of the locations. Research how long their journeys may have taken or any obstacles they may have encountered in their travels (culturally or geographically).

WORD STUDY (ORIGINAL LANGUAGE)

Brush up on your Greek and Hebrew and study the passage in the original language using an interlinear Bible.

READY TO DIVE IN?

Feel free to refer back to this list at any point, but now it's time to dive into the new HelloMornings study.

Here we go...

Cheering you on,

Kat Lee and the *HelloMornings.org* Team

God. Plan. Move.

A TOPICAL BIBLE STUDY

INTRODUCTION

ARE YOU FAMILIAR WITH THE THREE HELLO MORNINGS CORE COMPONENTS? They are: **God. Plan. Move.** These three core components are incredibly important to us! Over the years, we at this ministry have learned the value of seeking God first each day, aiming to plan our days around what He asks of us, and making decisions that move us toward a healthy lifestyle. We believe utilizing and developing these components is both life-changing and life-giving!

In this study, we'll spend six weeks looking at each of these three core components. We'll spend two weeks looking at the **God** component. Why should we want to meet with Him each day? In Week One, we'll talk about how we seek God because of *His character*. In Week Two, we'll look at our own character and discover why we, as God's creation, would need our Creator.

During the second set of two weeks in this study, we'll dive into **Plan.** What does the Bible say about planning, anyway? In our third week of this study, we'll look at what the Bible teaches about using our time and resources for His glory. In the fourth week we'll talk about applying planning skills to our lives and what the Bible says about living out God's will.

What does the Bible say about **Move?** God definitely has a call for each of us and it's important to treat our bodies in a way that we can do what He's asked. Week Five will discuss God's call for His children, and Week Six will examine what His Word says about making healthy and wise choices to enable us to obey His call.

Kat Lee, creator of Hello Mornings, likens the **God. Plan. Move.** components to a motorcycle. It's a simple analogy that really helps the concept sink in! God is our "engine" that empowers us to "go." Planning is the "handlebars" that steers our days in the direction He'd have us go. Moving (making healthy choices and taking care of ourselves) is the "wheels" that keep our bodies healthy enough to travel along His road for us.

The three components are all valuable parts of a life-giving morning routine!

Pray with me?

Father, I thank you greatly for each woman who opens this study and seeks your direction. Lord, please bless each reader as they develop their routine and look to your Word for clarification. Speak through your Word, Father, to each heart and give guidance on all three of the Hello Mornings components. Draw us close to you, Lord, as we seek to glorify you in **God. Plan. Move.** In Jesus' name!

Ali

WEEK 1, DAY 1: PSALM 143:8 AND LAMENTATIONS 3:21-25

I LOVE HEARING MY DAUGHTERS' VOICES! I'm thankful when they share their days, ask for advice, or just want to talk. I love the connection of communication! And I've tried to teach them this from the time they were little girls: just like I want to hear their voices and connect with them every day, God wants to do the same with us!

There is no better way to start our day than with meeting with God first. Psalm 143:8, our Hello Mornings core verse says, "Let me hear in the morning of your steadfast love, for in you I trust. Make me know the way I should go, for to you I lift up my soul." The rest of the day takes on a new perspective when we meet with Him first. Instead of looking at life through our limited earthly vision, we learn to see in the light of His steadfast love and perfect wisdom. He and His Word illuminate our paths (John 12:35-36 and Psalm 119:105) and God becomes the "true north" of our internal compass. As we grow nearer to Him and experience His immense love for us each day, our hearts change as we are transformed into His image. What a beautiful thing! (2 Corinthians 3:18)

Connecting with God benefits us greatly! Aspects of His character become more clear. One of my favorite attributes of God is His constant faithfulness. We can safely place our faith in the one who is ever-faithful to us. Jesus proved His faithfulness when He came to die for sinners and was obedient even to the point of death on a cross! (Romans 5:8 and Philippians 2:8) Yes, Jesus (the third person of our triune Godhead) is our Good Shepherd who laid His life down for us, His sheep. (John 10:11) We can take the easy, light yoke of our faithful Lord and go and grow His way. (Matthew 11:29-30)

Each day we can find new mercies through the evidence of His love, goodness, and grace. Our family, friends, and loved ones are extensions of His love. So are the strength to get through the hardest days, the comfort during grief, and the endurance to keep on keeping on. Our very breath each morning is a new mercy! Meeting with God each day equips us to both see and experience His mercies with vibrancy and a right posture of heart. What a joy that the Creator of the Universe longs to hear from and equip His children!

— **KEY VERSE** —

Let me hear in the morning of your steadfast love, for in you I trust. Let me know the way I should go, for to you I lift up my soul. (Psalm 143:8)

Hello mornings

God. Plan. Move.

GOD TIME

READ : Psalm 143:8 and Lamentations 3:21-25
WRITE : Psalm 143:8

....

....

....

REFLECT :
- Consider memorizing one or both of today's passages.
- What does John 10:27-30 tell you about His voice? Do you seek it daily?
- God changes us! Read commentary on 2 Corinthians 3:18. What did you learn?
- God gives us new mercies! Agree with Him and don't hold on to yesterday's failings.
- Look for God's love extended your way. Count your blessings and thank Him for His goodness and new mercies each day.

RESPOND :

....

....

....

....

....

PLAN TIME

THINGS TO DO (3-5 MAX) :

KEY EVENTS TODAY :

MOVE TIME

MORNING WATER ☐

B : _____

L : _____

D : _____

SNACK :

SIMPLE WORKOUT ☐

WEEK 1, DAY 2: MATTHEW 7:7-11

WHEN MY OLDEST WAS VERY LITTLE SHE ASKED FOR A PONY. Instead, my husband and I gave her a toy she'd been eyeing. She was thrilled with it even though she continued to want a pony for a long time. Years later, she realized that sharing an apartment with an equine wouldn't have been enjoyable for the pony nor for us! She learned that we knew what gifts were best for her, and that we gave from our loving wisdom.

Each day, we can approach God confidently knowing that He loves us and gives good and perfect gifts. (Hebrews 11:6, 1 John 4:8b, James 1:17) The Bible is full of promises of the good gifts that He gives! Eternal life to those who believe, the empowering of the Holy Spirit, and peace that passes understanding are a few. We can be certain to receive the things He has promised, while understanding that, like my daughter's request for a pony, sometimes we may ask for things He chooses not to give. God, in His perfect wisdom, gives what He knows is best for us: things that work for our eternal good and for His glory. God is a good Father!

Jesus tells His disciples in today's excerpt from the Sermon on the Mount to seek. I'm reminded of Psalm 27:8 where David says, *"You have said, 'Seek my face.' My heart says to you, 'Your face, Lord, do I seek.'"* Asking and seeking are similar, aren't they? But seeking takes things to a higher level. When my children play hide and seek, they actively look with desperation, expecting (needing!) to *find*. This is what Jesus wants of us. And the best thing? He promises that the seekers will be the finders!

Not only are we told to ask and seek, but we are told to knock. Each day we can come to God, knocking. Do you remember the Persistent Widow of Luke 18:1-8? She *kept coming* to an unjust judge, asking for justice against her adversary. The point? Persistence. It's an active demonstration of our faith! Our meetings with God prevent defeat. Like a baby learning to walk, we may stumble. It's in the getting up and going again that we gain strength and develop persistence.

Though the gifts God gives may or may not look exactly like we want, we can be assured of His goodness and love and that He always works what is best for us eternally. (Romans 8:28) We need just ask, seek, and knock.

— KEY VERSE —

Ask, and it will be given to you; seek, and you shall find; knock, and it will be opened to you. (Matthew 7:7)

Hello mornings

God. Plan. Move.

READ : Matthew 7:7-11
WRITE : Matthew 7:7

. . . .

REFLECT :
– Paraphrase today's passage in your own words.
– How are Matthew 7:11, 1 John 5:14-15, and Luke 22:42 related?
– Read Psalm 5:1-3. What can you learn? What do the words "and watch" imply?
– Research prayers of the Bible. What is God showing you about prayer?
– Pray to God: asking, seeking, and knocking all while trusting in His goodness.

RESPOND :

. . . .

THINGS TO DO (3-5 MAX) :

KEY EVENTS TODAY :

MORNING WATER ☐

B : _____
L : _____
D : _____

SNACK :

SIMPLE WORKOUT ☐

7

EVER HAVE ONE OF THOSE WEEKS when you fly from task to task with barely a moment to breathe in between? Sometimes, life can leave you feeling worn thin. This may be why I absolutely love Jesus' reminder to take His yoke and learn from Him. He promises spiritual rest!

I don't have to complete a long list of to-do's to be right with God. Instead, I can walk in freedom, tucked carefully inside His grace and love! Jesus explained in the Parable of the Wineskins (see Luke 5:33-38) that His new covenant of grace and faith wouldn't look like or fit with the Old Testament ways. The doctrine of grace isn't works based, friends. He is not impressed with my filling of spiritual checklists anyway! No, Jesus wants us to take His easy yoke and learn from Him. That's the key to spiritual rest.

Once, I had a wild horse. To train him to walk on a lead rope, my family loaned him to an experienced rancher. He tied my wild horse to a stronger, tame one. In a matter of weeks, the wild horse learned what it meant to follow. Jesus says in Matthew 11:29: *"Take my yoke upon you, and learn from me, for I am gentle and lowly in heart, and you will find rest for your souls."* We can take His yoke and tie ourselves side by side with Him. Yoked to Him, we learn His ways and rest in His strength.

Each day we have the choice to rest in His easy yoke. My day might be rushed and my to-do list long! Yet, I can have spiritual tranquility (what the Old Testament calls *shalom* in Hebrew) because I trust Him to lead the way, illuminate my path, meet my every need, give me His best, enable and equip me to do what He's called, and offer me grace along the way. Instead of striving and struggling on my own, I can be tied to Jesus who empowers me. What a great awareness to start our days with!

The Bible tells us that the Holy Spirit that Jesus sent to live in our hearts is our spiritual, living water that fills us to overflowing (John 4:14 and Romans 15:13). I don't come to The Well to work hard for my own spiritual satiety. Instead, I become a cup that runs over because of His fountain within my heart. I don't have to perform spiritual works to earn nor keep my salvation. In Him, I rest!

—  —

Come to me, all who labor and are heavy laden, and I will give you rest. (Matthew 11:28)

Hello mornings

God. Plan. Move.

READ : Matthew 11:27-30
WRITE : Matthew 11:28

....

....

....

REFLECT :
- Read the parable in Luke 5:33-38. How does this relate to today's reading?
- Research the word "yoke" in this passage. What did you learn?
- For more on resting from works, see Titus 3:5, Ephesians 2:8-9, and Romans 3:28.
- How could resting in Jesus' yoke each morning change your days?
- Pray. Ask God to help you rest from works and learn from Him. Thank Him for the new covenant of grace and faith.

RESPOND :

....

....

....

....

....

....

PLAN TIME

THINGS TO DO (3-5 MAX) :

KEY EVENTS TODAY :

MOVE TIME

MORNING WATER ☐

B : _____

L : _____

D : _____

SNACK :

SIMPLE WORKOUT ☐

WEEK 1, DAY 4: HEBREWS 4:11-16

HAVE YOU EVER HAD A FRIEND THAT *UNDERSTANDS* YOU? God has given me a few friends like that. Even though I'm an introvert, I love being with them, sharing my struggles, and gleaning from their wisdom. It's nice to have friends in whose company you can safely relax and share encouragement, help, and hope.

In the first part of today's passage, similar to yesterday's verses, the writer of Hebrews reminds his audience that Jesus gives us spiritual rest. We are reminded that no creature is hidden from God's sight; He knows our thoughts and our hearts. The beauty in that? We don't need to hide anything from Him. We can approach Him with confidence, standing forgiven and innocent because of Christ's blood! No matter what we've done and no matter our pasts. No matter how we treated our husband or talked to the kids or snapped when the other driver cut us off. *"If we confess our sins He is faithful and just to forgive us our sins and to cleanse us from all unrighteousness."* (1 John 1:9) Sin is ugly, but Christ's blood is beautiful!

Jesus, our most trustworthy friend (see John 15:13-15), understands every detail about us. We can come to Him daily, seeking His sympathy, His rest, and His help. Since our Savior is fully God and fully man, He understands our weaknesses and temptations. Remember, He was tempted, yet remained sinless. And being mighty, He can strengthen us with His empowering grace to help us through. Though I am weak, He is strong! We can confidently approach our friend, Jesus, with no shame or condemnation. We can relax in His safety.

We've been given an amazing opportunity to spend time each day with Christ as our Great High Priest! For me personally, I am awed that every morning, before the chaos of the day begins, before I am confronted with my hurts, struggles, or my sins, I can meet with Jesus and stand blameless before Him, laying my heart open. I can experience His love! It's such a simple thing, but it honestly gives me chills. Sisters, He knows we need Him! He knows our days have ups and downs that fill us with anxiety, stress, or even goodness and beauty. Our loving Priest is standing by, ready to help us and supply us with what we need, all while covering all our sin. Through Jesus' sacrifice, we have intimacy with God and fellowship with the one who knows and understands us so well!

— KEY VERSE —

Let us then with confidence draw near to the throne of grace, that we may receive mercy and find grace to help in time of need. (Hebrews 4:16)

Hello mornings

God. Plan. Move.

READ : Hebrews 4:11-16
WRITE : Hebrews 4:16

. . . .

. . . .

REFLECT :
- What stands out to you most in this passage?
- Read commentary on the "soul" and "spirit" mentioned in verse 12. What did you learn?
- Research the role of a high priest, then read Hebrews 5:1-10, 8:1-7, and 10:11-14 for insight into Jesus' role as high priest.
- Jesus is our friend! See *https://www.desiringgod.org/articles/what-a-friend-we-have-in-jesus*
- Approach God confidently today. Thank Him for always being available!

RESPOND :

. . . .

. . . .

. . . .

. . . .

PLAN TIME

THINGS TO DO (3-5 MAX) :

KEY EVENTS TODAY :

MOVE TIME

MORNING WATER ☐

B : _____
L : _____
D : _____

SNACK :

SIMPLE WORKOUT ☐

WEEK 1, DAY 5: PSALM 91:1-4, 9-10, AND 14-16

THE EARTHQUAKE WAS A TOTAL SURPRISE! My husband and I had just moved to Washington state when the 6.8 magnitude quake hit. The morning started as usual until the earth groaned in exclamation and the jumping buildings echoed back a reply. It was so loud, I initially thought there had been an explosion. But realizing what was happening, I sought a safe place in the room for us to ride the jerking earth.

There are times in life when we need physical refuge. Whether it's from an earthquake, a storm, or even abuse or attack, a refuge offers us safe shelter from physical trouble. But we need a safe *spiritual* hideaway, too. Sisters, we have three enemies. One is Satan, who comes to kill, steal, and destroy (John 10:10). I don't love to focus on Satan, but we must understand that he is real and has been ultimately defeated. God equips us to fight him (Ephesians 6:10-18) and offers us a safe, strong shelter (Psalm 91:4). Our other enemies? The world around us, and our very own selves.

"Are we in danger from visible or invisible enemies? God is our refuge, to whom we may flee, and in whom we may be safe. Have we work to do, a warfare to accomplish, and sufferings to endure? God is our strength to bear us up..."—Benson Commentary

God as refuge reminds me of the water from the spring of Gihon that flowed from outside the city of Jerusalem into the interior, protected part. Water offered physical salvation during enemy attacks. On the last day of the Feast of Booths, (see John 7:37-39) , the water was collected at the pool of Siloam and poured into a basin that flowed over the Temple altar. The Jews associated Siloam's pool with the outpouring of the Holy Spirit—just what Jesus referred to when He claimed that we could come to Him to drink. We can come to Him to drink and also *"abide in the shadow of the Almighty."* (Psalm 91:1) How refreshing!

Friends, the enemy is a liar and an attacker, the world is a rough place, and we can be cruel even to ourselves. But Jesus offers us His Holy Spirit to help us and He gives us sustaining, life-giving refuge! The winds and storm can whirl around us, but we are safe under the shelter of His wings. Without Him, we are tossed to fro by the storms, but holding fast to Jesus, our refuge, we can have inexplicable peace.

— KEY VERSE —

He will cover you with his pinions, and under his wings you will find refuge; his faithfulness is a shield and buckler. (Psalm 91:4)

Hello mornings

God. Plan. Move.

READ : Psalm 91:1-4, 9-10, and 14-16
WRITE : Psalm 91:4

. . . .

. . . .

REFLECT :
- God is talking in verses 14-16. What does God do? What should man do?
- Does this Psalm promise nothing bad will happen to us? Research verses 9 and 10.
- Fighting one of the three enemies? See Ephesians 6:10-18, Romans 12:2, 1 John 4:4, Romans 8:1, John 16:33, and Romans 8:35-39.
- Read Matthew 14:25-31. What insight might you gain in relation to today's passage?
- Look up the hymn "Til the Storm Passes By." Thank God for being your refuge.

RESPOND :

. . . .

. . . .

. . . .

. . . .

PLAN TIME

THINGS TO DO (3-5 MAX) :

KEY EVENTS TODAY :

MOVE TIME

MORNING WATER ☐

B : _____

L : _____

D : _____

SNACK :

SIMPLE WORKOUT ☐

WEEK 2, DAY 1: JOHN 4:7-14

THE *NEW YORK TIMES* BESTSELLER, *Catch Me If You Can: The True Story of a Real Fake* reveals the story of Frank W. Abagnale. Before the age of 21, Abagnale forged and cashed over $2.5 million in checks, impersonated a medical resident, a lawyer, and a college professor. He posed as a co-pilot for Pan Am airlines. We read a biography like this with awe, wondering how anyone could circumvent the truth and get away with it.

Abagnale's life is full of "stranger-than-fiction" escapades, but the basic fact is he lived a lie. This isn't unique to Abagnale. As we focus on today's verses, we see that the Samaritan woman, commonly referred to as "the woman at the well," was also trying to hide the truth of her life. The conversation between this lost and hurting woman and the divine Son of God changed the course of her life forever.

Jesus encountered this woman at Jacob's Well. In this rare conversation between a Jewish man and a Samaritan woman, Jesus drew her attention to two things: His gift and His person. He said to her *"if you knew the gift of God and who it is that is saying to you, 'Give me a drink'"* (verse 10) to shift her attention to her own need. The truth was that Jesus didn't need water as much as the woman needed Jesus. He used the word dᐤrean, which is a gift "transferred freely by one person to another." This woman had no idea that she was in the presence of the Son of God who was offering her the free gift of Himself. She was standing face-to-face with truth but couldn't understand it.

Her response is a human one: *"Sir, you have nothing to draw water with"* (verse 11). She didn't understand Christ's words at this point, thinking only of filling a jar with well water. Jesus continued to offer her truth, contrasting her ideas of earthly well water to the life-giving water that only He could provide.

Jesus came to give each of us water that would *"become in [us] a spring of water welling up to eternal life"* (verse 14). He knew this woman was spiritually thirsty and had unsuccessfully attempted to satisfy her inner thirst. (Read verses 16-19.) He knows the same about you and me. Take some time to enjoy His life-giving water by reading His Word today.

— **KEY VERSE** —

...but whoever drinks of the water that I will give him will never be thirsty again. (John 4:14a)

Hello mornings

God. Plan. Move.

READ : John 4:7-14
WRITE : John 4:14a

....

....

....

REFLECT :
- Read more about Jacob's Well: *https://www.biblestudytools.com/dictionary/jacobs-well/*
- What have you substituted in your life and heart for living water? Confess this to the Lord.
- Have a conversation with your "younger self." What would you say about avoiding spiritual thirst? How can you prevent this in the future?
- Read John 7:37. Why is Jesus using the example of water again?
- Listen to the song "Living Water." *https://www.youtube.com/watch?v=96s50957u4Y*

RESPOND :

....

....

....

....

....

....

PLAN TIME

THINGS TO DO (3-5 MAX) :

KEY EVENTS TODAY :

MOVE TIME

MORNING WATER ☐

B : _____

L : _____

D : _____

SNACK :

SIMPLE WORKOUT ☐

WEEK 2, DAY 2: PSALM 46:10; LUKE 10:38-42

POWER OUTAGES ARE A COMMON OCCURRENCE ON OUR STREET. First, it's the unexpected flicker of the lights. We hold our breath and hope it's just a momentary blip. When the inevitable happens, our world goes dark. I'm always amazed that it also goes quiet. You don't realize how much noise you have around you until it's gone.

In those quiet, dark hours, there is little we can do, particularly if there are storms brewing. Unless my husband is home to manually lift the garage door, I'm trapped. We must wait in the quiet stillness for the rigs to come down the street to repair the damage.

These hours of forced quiet remind me that God wants us to do this daily. In Psalm 46:10 He says, *"Be still, and know that I am God."* It often takes a power outage for me to "be still."

It is significant that Jesus taught us this lesson in stillness through the eyes and hearts of two women. The sisters, Mary and Martha of Bethany, were close friends of Jesus. So close, in fact, that the Son of God showed up at their house. Martha welcomed Him and must have gone straight into Martha Stewart mode. She was so caught up in serving that she didn't bother to *"be still."* But her sister Mary was sitting at the feet of Jesus. We can take it from Martha's frustrated plea for help that Mary didn't lift a finger to assist in serving their guests.

Jesus gave Martha a quick answer, but I doubt it was what she wanted or expected. He tells her *"one thing is necessary"* and *"Mary has chosen the good portion"* (verse 42). Mary demonstrated the need for us to "be still" at the feet of Jesus. While His words might seem harsh to us, Jesus took time to stop and teach this dear woman a valuable lesson. He did not dismiss her but wanted Martha to understand that all her service without "the one thing" was only going to result in total frustration. She was going to have a personal power outage!

In our fast-paced, high-tech world, being still requires a ready heart. We must switch off, stop, and sit. Ask yourself:

Am I ready to hear and obey God's Word with an open heart today?

Am I ready to put total faith in Him today?

If your answer isn't an honest "yes" to these questions, spend some time with Jesus and find the *"one thing"* He has for you today.

— KEY VERSE —

But the Lord answered her, "Martha, Martha, you are anxious and troubled about many things, but one thing is necessary. Mary has chosen the good portion," (Luke 10:41-42)

Hello mornings

God. Plan. Move.

GOD TIME

READ : Psalm 46:10; Luke 10:38-42
WRITE : Luke 10:41-42

REFLECT :
- What one major distraction keeps you from hearing from God? Confess this to Him today.
- What changes do you need to make in your morning routine to have time for being still?
- Read about what is means to have a quiet heart in Isaiah 30:15, I Peter 3:4 and I Kings 8:61.
- Listen to Myquillyn Smith's podcast on creating a morning space: *https://www.hellomornings.org/hm-36-create-a-cozy-morning-space-with-myquillyn-smith/*
- Read Psalm 27:4 and Philippians 3:13-14. How do these verses relate to today's lesson?

RESPOND :

PLAN TIME

THINGS TO DO (3-5 MAX) :

KEY EVENTS TODAY :

MOVE TIME

MORNING WATER ☐

B : _____

L : _____

D : _____

SNACK :

SIMPLE WORKOUT ☐

WEEK 2, DAY 3: LUKE 18:1-8

TODAY'S READING IS A PARABLE RECORDED ONLY BY LUKE, THE GENTILE DOCTOR.
This parable reveals more than a determined widow. Jesus was contrasting His Father, the righteous judge who rewards our persistent prayer with an unrighteous judge.

Jesus taught His disciples about His future kingdom in Luke 17:20-37. This parable follows as a further elaboration on how we are to live as His children, waiting for His return. God expects us to continually pray and live with tenacious faith.

Jesus paints a word picture to illustrate His point. Looking at the characters of the narrative, we get an understanding of what is going on in their hearts. The judge, *"neither feared God nor respected man"* (verse 2). This calloused man refused to do his job as a judge: administer justice. The widow continually showed up in his court because she needed the intervention of the law. All we know is that she repeatedly appeared and made her request. The story does not say she was disrespectful or rude but persistently asked that her case be heard. Her need must have been great because she doesn't give up until the judge gives in.

The parable shifts when Jesus asked, *"And will not God give justice to his elect, who cry to him day and night?"* (verse 7). This is a "how much more?" question. Jesus is not saying God is like the unjust judge, administering reluctant justice, but He *"will give justice to them [His elect] speedily"* (verse 8) because He loves to bless His children. If an unjust judge will grant someone's request, how much more will God bestow justice when we are prayerfully persistent?

We all have requests that we continually bring before God. It's easy to ask God to bless a meal or give us a safe commute to the office. It becomes hard when we have deep unspeakable needs that we bring to God day in and day out. I have some requests that I really want to stop bringing before God because perseverance in prayer is tough and painfully tests my faith. My heart hurts because there has been no response from my Heavenly Father yet. My husband keeps encouraging me to pray a little longer and wait for God's answer.

Jesus wrapped up the parable with the Big Question. He asks, *"when the Son of Man comes, will he find faith on earth?"* (verse 8) Reframing the question, we can ask ourselves, "When Jesus returns, will I be standing before Him as an example of faith because I have been persistently praying?

—  KEY VERSE —

And will not God give justice to his elect, who cry to him day and night? (Luke 18:7a)

Hello mornings
God. Plan. Move.

READ : Luke 18:1-8
WRITE : Luke 18:7a

. . . .

. . . .

. . . .

REFLECT :
  – Create a chart contrasting God to the unrighteous judge. What did you learn?
  – Look up the word *always* in verse 1 using *https://biblehub.com/interlinear/luke/18.htm*.
    Why do you think Jesus used this word?
  – Is prayer your last resort in a situation or your first response? Reflect on your response.
  – What changes do you need to make in your prayer life to become an "always" petitioner?
  – Reflect on this: *God is always working on a purpose we cannot see.* -John O. Reid

RESPOND :

. . . .

. . . .

. . . .

. . . .

. . . .

PLAN TIME

THINGS TO DO (3-5 MAX) :

MOVE TIME

MORNING WATER ☐

B : _____
L : _____
D : _____

KEY EVENTS TODAY :

SNACK :

SIMPLE WORKOUT ☐

WEEK 2, DAY 4: ROMANS 8:26-39; EPHESIANS 6:17

I HAD TO TAKE A FOREIGN LANGUAGE IN COLLEGE. It made perfect sense for me to take German. After all, I had two years of German in high school, so I arrogantly thought I knew the language. If I attended the lectures, I was confident I would be prepared to read and understand the week's passages.

Six weeks into the first course, I realized that I had exhausted all my knowledge. I wasn't just wading in unfamiliar territory, I was drowning! I attended the lectures, leaving with the same confidence that I could handle the week's readings, but not a day passed that I didn't get discouraged and want to give up because the passages were becoming more and more difficult to understand. I learned I had to study every day.

More often than I'd like to confess, my walk with God is like my study of German. I go to worship and leave fired up that I can handle anything that Satan chunks at me. But by Wednesday, doubts start to creep in. When Friday rolls around, I can often be so discouraged that I just want to give up.

Our God knew we'd need a sword to fight off the enemy, so He gave us His Word. This essential *"sword of the Spirit"* (Ephesians 6:17) includes the dynamic, life-giving passage in Romans 8. It's chocked full answers to the questions we ask when we are in doubt or discouraged. *God, are you for me? God, do you still love me today? God, why do I keep remembering something I did two months ago that didn't please You? Why do I feel condemned by this?*

The promises of God answer these doubts and fears. Paul tells us *"in all these things we are more than conquerors through him who loved us" (verse 37)*. We are "super conquerors," completely and overwhelmingly victorious because of Jesus Christ. To be a conqueror, we need our sword. A good soldier didn't run into battle never having used his weapon. He'd spend many hours using his sword in mock skirmishes, visualizing how he'd attack an enemy. Unless he'd practiced, he had no "battle instinct." He was useless in the fight.

We need daily practice with our sword, the Word of God, to have battle instinct against Satan. We must study, even when we are discouraged because the verses are hard to understand. When we are ready to throw up our hands and cry, "I give up! This is too hard!" God reminds us that *"we are more than conquerors."* (verse 37)

— KEY VERSE —

...and take the helmet of salvation, and the sword of the Spirit, which is the word of God, (Ephesians 6:17)

Hello mornings

God. Plan. Move.

READ : Romans 8:26-39; Ephesians 6:17
WRITE : Ephesians 6:17

....

....

....

REFLECT :
– Romans 8:36 is a reference to Psalm 44:22. How would you explain this?
– Read Romans 8:31-35. What did you learn about God's view of discouragement?
– How can Joshua 1:9, Psalm 27:14, and John 16:33 help you overcome discouragement?
– Write a personal paraphrase of Romans 8:37-39 to help you connect with the text.
– Read Romans 8:37-39 again. Underline the positive components and circle the negative.

RESPOND :

....

....

....

....

....

....

PLAN TIME

THINGS TO DO (3-5 MAX) :

KEY EVENTS TODAY :

MOVE TIME

MORNING WATER ☐

B : _____

L : _____

D : _____

SNACK :

SIMPLE WORKOUT ☐

WEEK 2, DAY 5: PHILIPPIANS 3:8-16

OUR FRIEND STEVE IS A CYCLIST. He isn't a casual rider. Steve is a "let's hit the hills and ride for hours" guy. For the past two years, he's biked across the state of Oklahoma in temperatures that could fry eggs on a sidewalk. Surviving distance rides in rain, cold, and excessive heat, Steve is a living example of what it means to "press on." He and his cycling partners encourage each other to go one more mile, pedal up one more hill, or keep on a trail one more hour.

Much like a band of dedicated cyclists, Paul exhorts the Philippians to *"press on toward the goal for the prize of the upward call of God..."* (verse 14) We all are painfully aware that life has one more load of laundry or one more sleepless night walking a crying baby. The challenge is to recalibrate our daily life to seek the *"prize of the upward call of God."* God's call on our lives is the prize whether it is home-schooling, deciding if a client qualifies for a loan, or serving as a caregiver to an aging parent. We have each been called by the Creator to partner with Him in kingdom work.

Paul wrote these words from prison. While he could assuredly say that he *"suffered the loss of all things,"* (verse 8) his external surroundings were not impacting his internal confidence in Christ. To Paul, all that mattered was to "know him and the power of his resurrection." (verse 10) Paul didn't have a casual acquaintance with God. He didn't just pray from time to time, begging God to help him in a crisis. Paul knew God because of their daily, intimate relationship. He spent time with God, the mark of a mature Christian.

Steve didn't start his cycling hobby by making a 30-mile ride the first day. To become a seasoned cyclist, a rider must start with short riding sessions, increasing their time and distance slowly. A young rider should ride with a more experienced cyclist to learn how to shift gears, coast down steep hills, and stop without sailing over the handlebars. Passionate riders consult experts for help and advice on cycling.

Becoming a mature Christian is much like becoming a seasoned cyclist. It takes time to learn about God, get past the acquaintance phase, and really know Him. Paul couldn't live the Christian life alone and we can't either. We need mature Believers to walk beside us to teach us how to walk with God as our own band of dedicated learners.

— KEY VERSE —

But one thing I do: forgetting what lies behind and straining forward to what lies ahead, I press on toward the goal for the prize of the upward call of God in Christ Jesus. (Philippians 3:13b-14)

Hello mornings

God. Plan. Move.

READ : Philippians 3:8-16
WRITE : Philippians 3:13b-14

REFLECT :
- What is one goal you accomplished in the past six months that required sacrifice?
- How does Luke 9:62 relate to today's verses?
- Who is an example of one who "presses on" in the Christian life? Journal about them today.
- Read James 1:21-22 and Ephesians 4:22-24. Infuse these truths into your plan time today.
- Research spiritual disciplines: *https://www.gotquestions.org/spiritual-disciplines.html*

RESPOND :

PLAN TIME

THINGS TO DO (3-5 MAX) :

KEY EVENTS TODAY :

MOVE TIME

MORNING WATER ☐

B : _____
L : _____
D : _____

SNACK :

SIMPLE WORKOUT ☐

WEEK 3, DAY 1: MATTHEW 25:1-13

BEING A WOMAN OF SHORT STATURE, I anticipated that my first time going into labor might begin earlier than the average 40 weeks. So, a month before our son's due date, I started making checklists, packing bags, and making sure that every day when I left work things were in order should I not return. I could not plan the day or the hour of my son's birth, but I could maintain a spirit of readiness.

When it was all said and done, my firstborn came via cesarean section at 39 weeks and 6 days after 36 hours of labor–neither early nor in any of the scenarios I had seriously considered in my head. But our bags were packed, the car seat was ready, and we had the number to call when my water broke. As much as one can plan for the unpredictable, we were prepared.

Jesus told the crowds and His disciples that *"the kingdom of heaven will be like ten virgins who took their lamps and went to meet the bridegroom. Five of them were foolish [thoughtless, silly, and careless], and five were wise [far-sighted, practical, and sensible]"* (Matthew 25:1-2, AMP). The wise virgins, or bridesmaids, took flasks of oil with their lamps, for they knew that the bridegroom might tarry or be delayed and the oil already in their lamps might prove insufficient.

> *The heart is the vessel, which it is our good wisdom to get furnished; for, out of a good treasure there, good things must be brought; … Grace is the oil which we must have in this vessel; … Our light must shine before men in good works, … with an eye to what is before us."*
> —Matthew Henry

If we, as believers, desire to use our time and resources wisely for God's glory, then we, too, need to be wise and adopt a spirit of watchfulness and readiness. Psalm 119:15 reminds us to *"meditate on your precepts and fix [our] eyes on your ways."* Having all of Scripture at our disposal, by the Holy Spirit we can become kingdom-minded. Jesus Himself—the Author and Finisher of our faith—was able to endure the cross *"for the joy set before Him,"* and it is upon Him we are to fix our eyes (Hebrews 12:2, NASB).

When we are consistently in the Word of God and spending time communicating with Him, we will be ready to glorify Him when He unexpectedly brings people or situations into our days. And because we are not of this world, we can also orient our priorities in light of His return.

— KEY VERSE —

Watch therefore, for you know neither the day nor the hour. (Matthew 25:13)

Hello mornings

God. Plan. Move.

READ : Matthew 25:1-13
WRITE : Matthew 25:13

....

....

REFLECT :
- Observe the differences between the characters involved in the parable of the ten virgins.
- Research ancient Jewish wedding customs for context (*https://www.biblestudytools.com/ commentaries/revelation/related-topics/the-jewish-wedding-analogy.html*).
- Read the parable of the weeds (Matthew 13:24-30). How does this relate to today's passage?
- Look up 1 Peter 3:15. What is this verse calling us to be ready to do?
- Pray that God would make you more like the wise virgins this week.

RESPOND :

....

....

....

....

....

PLAN TIME

THINGS TO DO (3-5 MAX) :

KEY EVENTS TODAY :

MOVE TIME

MORNING WATER ☐

B : _____

L : _____

D : _____

SNACK :

SIMPLE WORKOUT ☐

WEEK 3, DAY 2: EPHESIANS 2:8-10; COLOSSIANS 3:17

I LOVE THE WIDOWS IN OUR CHURCH; I am always amazed by how loving and sacrificial these women are. Though they have undoubtedly had others pour into them throughout their lifetimes, one could argue that they have served, and now it is their turn to be served. But, more often than not, I observe them serving God faithfully: tithing generously, sewing blankets for newborns, attending every wedding and baby shower even though they don't always know the younger ladies, sending birthday cards or notes of encouragement, baking cookies for fellowships, and (most impactfully) offering to pray for others with the quiet certainty that they will follow through.

I want to spend more time with these women. I desire to learn from them and to imitate them as they imitate Christ. It is so tempting to look at our busy lives and think, "Once I get past this stage, I will have more time for that ministry," but every season has its challenges and its unique opportunities. I need to be more diligent about asking for His wisdom as to what I say yes to, for that is the heart of Spirit-led planning.

God explicitly tells us that our salvation is not borne of our attempts to try and keep the law, but it is His undeserved, gracious gift to us borne of His remarkable compassion and favor in drawing us to Christ (Ephesians 2:8-9, AMP). *"For we are his workmanship, created in Christ Jesus for good works, **which God prepared beforehand** that we should walk in them"* (v. 10, emphasis added). I am simply in awe when I think of how God prearranged the different stages in my life and how I can be used for His glory during them.

> *"Works are 'good' only when they spring from the principle of love to God. Faith and love in the heart are the essential elements of all true obedience. ...Good works have the **glory of God as their object**; and they have revealed the will of God as their only rule. Good works are an **expression of gratitude** in the believer's heart."*—Easton's Bible Dictionary, emphasis added

When we can let go of our need to do good works to earn God's favor, we can be transformed into master works of art who seek God's will in dependence on Him and strive to live out the good works He has prepared for us for the season we are in today–out of an overflow of the thankfulness in our hearts and all for His glory.

— KEY VERSE —

And whatever you do, in word or deed, do everything in the name of the Lord Jesus, giving thanks to God the Father through him. (Colossians 3:17)

Hello mornings

God. Plan. Move.

READ : Ephesians 2:8-10; Colossians 3:17
WRITE : Colossians 3:17

REFLECT :
- Highlight the gifts or actions that stem from God; in a different color, highlight the believer's.
- Read Romans 1:20. As His workmanship, how can you reflect God's invisible attributes today?
- Look up the definition for grace in a concordance or lexicon; meditate on God's grace to you.
- Make two columns labeled "For God's glory" and "For my glory." Write down some of the good works you've done this week and prayerfully evaluate which column they fall under.
- Memorize today's key verse.

RESPOND :

PLAN TIME

THINGS TO DO (3-5 MAX) :

KEY EVENTS TODAY :

MOVE TIME

MORNING WATER ☐

B : _____
L : _____
D : _____

SNACK :

SIMPLE WORKOUT ☐

WEEK 3, DAY 3: EPHESIANS 5:15-17; PSALM 90:12

"... Love one another earnestly from a pure heart, since you have been born again, not of perishable seed but of imperishable, through the living and abiding word of God; for 'All flesh is like grass and all its glory like the flower of grass. The grass withers, and the flower falls, but the word of the Lord remains forever.' And this word is the good news that was preached to you." (1 Peter 1:22b-25)

I love learning modern hymns. There is one we have sung several times at our church that still humbles me every time I sing it. It reminds me that my worth is not found in my material possessions, nor in my strength; not in my skill, nor in my reputation; not in my wins or losses, my pride or my shame. For me, the driving point of the hymn is when it leads me to the truth that my value has already been fixed by the precious blood of Christ that paid my ransom at the cross.

When I think of the price that my dear Savior paid to redeem me from the power of sin and death that I might be adopted into the Father's family as His Son's coheir, it is staggering (Galatians 4:5). And when He then commands me to *"walk circumspectly, not as fools but as wise, **redeeming the time**,"* I find myself cut to the heart (Ephesians 5:15-16, NKJV, emphasis added).

The word "redeem" is translated from the Greek root word *exagorazō*. When used in reference to Christ's redemption of us, it means "by payment of a price to recover from the power of another, to ransom, buy off." But when used in this Ephesians passage, it refers to our own selves as the redeemers: "to make **wise and sacred use of every opportunity** for doing good, so that zeal and well-doing are as it were the purchase money by which we make the time our own" (Thayer's Greek Lexicon, emphasis added).

Psalm 90:12 reminds us that we need the eternal God to *"[t]each us to number our days that we may get a heart of wisdom."* We are like the summer flowers that wither and die; our time on earth is so very, very short in light of eternity. When we approach our time as precious to us and to the Lord, and we seek to understand His will for how we use our time, we can be wise in how we, as good stewards, spend the hours, days, weeks, and years He has given us.

—  —

KEY VERSE

Therefore do not be foolish, but understand what the will of the Lord is. (Ephesians 5:17)

Hello mornings

God. Plan. Move.

READ : Ephesians 5:15-17; Psalm 90:12
WRITE : Ephesians 5:17

....

....

REFLECT :
- Watch the video for the hymn "My Worth Is Not in What I Own" (*https://youtu.be/05jKxv8ApuI*).
- For more on redemption, look up Galatians 3:13 and 4:4-7 and Titus 2:14.
- Journal about what you have been redeemed from and redeemed for.
- Read Psalm 90:12-14. What does a heart of wisdom lead to?
- Pray that God would enable you to "make wise and sacred use of every opportunity" today

RESPOND :

....

....

....

....

....

PLAN TIME

THINGS TO DO (3-5 MAX) :

KEY EVENTS TODAY :

MOVE TIME

MORNING WATER ☐

B : _____

L : _____

D : _____

SNACK :

SIMPLE WORKOUT ☐

WEEK 3, DAY 4: MATTHEW 25:14-30

A FEW YEARS AGO, dear friends of ours were called to pastor a church in the southern part of our state. One of the many areas of service they had become involved with at our church was our nursery. For a few years, we had struggled with finding a consistent person or team to coordinate this ministry; these two saw a need and jumped right in.

When they announced their impending move, I felt the Spirit leading me to offer to step in as coordinator. Honestly, I felt a bit like I was on the edge of a precipice. I knew that I had been poured into by countless saints; now God was calling me to take this step of faith and take on a larger role than I ever had before.

It is easy to have thoughts of inadequacy—to look at our capabilities and think them small compared to those who have gone before us. In Matthew 25, Jesus uses the parable of the talents to remind us that all that we have—our possessions, time, relationships, our strengths, and even our weaknesses—are His. We are but slaves to Christ our Master, for we have been bought with the price of His precious blood. As His servants, we are called to be *"good stewards of the manifold grace of God"* (1 Peter 4:10, NASB).

What really floors me about this passage is that, of the three servants, each one had at least one talent. When I read this parable, I tend to focus on the servant who received five talents and am distracted by why he should get to start out with so much. When I focus instead on the truth that even one talent is more than I could ever deserve, I see just how weighty a thing it is to be entrusted with so much. As Matthew Henry says, *"For the truth is, the more we do for God, the more we are indebted to him for making use of us, and enabling us, for his service."*

To the good and faithful servant, Christ says, *"Well done,"* and *"You have been faithful in handling this small amount, so now I will give you many more responsibilities"* (Matthew 25:21, NLT). Our hearts might say, *"Well, that doesn't sound like a very good deal for me!"* But our Servant King also says, *"For to everyone who has will more be given, and he will have an **abundance**"* (v. 29, emphasis added). God will supply all our needs, we need but respond to His call and invest ourselves for His kingdom.

— KEY VERSE —

For to everyone who has [and values his blessings and gifts from God, and has used them wisely], more will be given, and [he will be richly supplied so that] he will have an abundance ... (Matthew 25:29a, AMP)

Hello mornings

God. Plan. Move.

READ : Matthew 25:14-30
WRITE : Matthew 25:29a

. . . .

. . . .

REFLECT :

- Compare and contrast the three servants in this parable.
- Read 1 Timothy 5:13. What tends to happen when we let idleness creep into our lives?
- Look up 1 Peter 4:7-11 in the NASB. What is the purpose of the gifts we have been given?
- Make a list of at least five gifts you have been given in each of the areas of time, money, possessions, relationships, and abilities.
- Pray about ways God can enable you to use those gifts for His glory.

RESPOND :

. . . .

. . . .

. . . .

PLAN TIME

THINGS TO DO (3-5 MAX) :

KEY EVENTS TODAY :

MOVE TIME

MORNING WATER ☐

B : _____

L : _____

D : _____

SNACK :

SIMPLE WORKOUT ☐

WEEK 3, DAY 5: LUKE 12:13-21

AS AN ADULT, I was surprised to attend wedding ceremonies and hear the answers to the pastor's questions during the declaration of intent. Instead of hearing the bride and groom answer "I do," I began to hear couples answering "I will." I loved that subtle switch from "*I do* promise to love and cherish" to "*I will* promise." Each morning, we either renew our vow to pursue our spouses with a Christlike love, or our promise momentarily falls by the wayside. I cannot biblically love my husband in my own strength; my desire to love him can only be carried out through my pursuit of loving God more.

When I am tempted to rely on my own self-righteousness, I need to remember that I can only produce eternal fruit when I am abiding in Christ (John 15:4). In the parable in Luke 12, after the Lord blessed the rich man with fertile land, he began to worry about where he would store the abundance of his harvest. *"And he said, 'I will do this: I will tear down my barns and build larger ones, and there I will store all my grain and my goods.'"* (Luke 12:18, emphasis added)

We find the rich man basking in his accomplishments and stewing over what to do with his bounty rather than praising God for His gifts and asking Him for wisdom in how to best use them. The word translated into the phrase "I will do" in verse 18 finds it root in the same word that is translated into "make" in Matthew 5:36: *"And do not take an oath by your head, for you cannot make one hair white or black."* We are not truly the ones who bring about increase; there is only one Author, Creator, and Sustainer, *"…for He causes His sun to rise on the evil and the good, and sends rain on the righteous and the unrighteous"* (Matthew 5:45).

How easy it is to be like the rich man and say, "*I will* make this happen. *I will* work hard and enjoy the fruits of my labor," but that would make me foolish just like him. Each morning is a new chance to seek the Lord and thank Him for His blessings and a new opportunity to ask for strength to use our time and resources for His plans and purposes for His glory. We would all do well to take time each morning, not to focus on "What will I do?" but on "What does God want to do with me?"

—  KEY VERSE —

So is the one who lays up treasure for himself and is not rich toward God. (Luke 12:21)

Hello mornings

God. Plan. Move.

GOD TIME

READ : Luke 12:13-21
WRITE : Luke 12:21

. . . .

. . . .

REFLECT :

– Read Ecclesiastes 5:10-12. How do these verses describe the rich man in today's parable?
– Look up 1 Timothy 6:6-10 and 17-19. How can riches lead God's people astray?
– According to the 1 Timothy passage, what are Believers called to set their hope on?
– What does today's parable say about God and how he views our lives on earth?
– How can you seek to be rich in your relationship with God this week?

RESPOND :

. . . .

. . . .

. . . .

. . . .

. . . .

PLAN TIME

THINGS TO DO (3-5 MAX) :

KEY EVENTS TODAY :

MOVE TIME

MORNING WATER ☐

B : _____

L : _____

D : _____

SNACK :

SIMPLE WORKOUT ☐

WEEK 4, DAY 1: ECCLESIASTES 12:31; MATTHEW 22:34-40

I STRUGGLE WITH PLANNING, so I accepted this topic as an opportunity for God to work in my life to develop this habit. I know God has a purpose for me in keeping with who He is and what He wills, but before I strategize how to accomplish it, I must first seek Him and His will. Jesus said, *"love the Lord your God with all your heart and with all your soul and with all your mind"* (Matthew 22:37). I do this by setting aside time to embrace God's Word, connect with Him, and obey His commands. In doing so, I align myself more and more with God, and uncover His purpose for me in His will.

Embrace God's Word—read it, study it, adopt it. Concerning His Word, God says, *"it shall not return to me empty, but it shall accomplish that which I purpose, and shall succeed in the thing for which I sent it"* (Isaiah 55:11). What a powerful promise! Through the power of the Holy Spirit living in you, God will illumine the truths in His Word, He will reveal who you are in Him, and He will accomplish His purpose in you. Decide today to put God first by making time for His Word.

Connect with God—submit to Him in prayer. The psalmist writes, *"The Lord is near to all who call on him, to all who call on him in truth"* (Psalm 145:18). Mother Teresa echoes this, *". . . Prayer is putting oneself in the hands of God, at His disposition, and listening to His voice in the depth of our hearts."* In prayer, devote heart, soul, and mind to God's purpose, and He will fashion a unique purpose for you that will fulfill His. Decide today to put God first by making time to pray.

Obey His Commands—demonstrate your love for God. God's commands have our best interest in mind, and they equip us to live out God's will. King Solomon wrote, *". . . Fear God and keep his commandments, for this is the whole duty of man"* (Ecclesiastes 12:13). The more we love God through obedience, the better we understand the purpose of His commands. Obedience brings us further in line with God's purpose, and as we plan to fulfill His purpose, we understand our own. Decide today to trust God by obeying Him.

Knowing and doing God's will takes precedence in all things. Having sought Him first, we are ready to work with God to plan how best to live for Him.

— KEY VERSE —

And he said to him, "You shall love the Lord your God with all your heart and with all your soul and with all your mind." (Matthew 22:37)

Hello mornings

God. Plan. Move.

READ : Ecclesiastes 12:31; Matthew 22:34-40
WRITE : Matthew 22:37

....

....

REFLECT :
- Locate The Big Bible Study Idea List found on pages viii-xi of this study. Pick a new tip or tool to try this week.
- Write down your personal paraphrase of Matthew 22:34-40. What did you learn?
- Listen to Hello Mornings Podcast, HM 22, at *www.hellomornings.org/podcast*.
- Struggling with prayer? Practice by praying Scripture. Try Ephesians 3:14-21.
- What steps can you take today to love God better?

RESPOND :

....

....

....

....

....

PLAN TIME

THINGS TO DO (3-5 MAX) :

KEY EVENTS TODAY :

MOVE TIME

MORNING WATER ☐

B : _____

L : _____

D : _____

SNACK :

SIMPLE WORKOUT ☐

WEEK 4, DAY 2: MATTHEW 6:25-33

FULLY CONVINCED THAT MY LIFE IS TO REVOVLE AROUND GOD AND FOLLOW HIS WILL, how I plan my days is an indicator of how well I put hands and feet on this conviction. Jesus instructs us, *". . . seek first the kingdom of God and his righteousness, and all these things will be added to you"* (Matthew 6:33). Considering this, God wants me to plan, prioritize, and trust Him as I work to do His will.

Plan. A plan creates a pathway for doing God's will. In Matthew 6:33, the first word, *"Seek,"* indicates action. Seeking is done with intention; it requires planning. Working with God, I steward my personality, talents and God-given gifts to effectively fulfill His will and purpose for my future. Jeff Lowdy, a strategist for non-profits lists a plan's components: process, strategy, accountability, and communication. Let's consider how we can use this as we plan to serve God.

- Process: I establish a vision and a mission statement to steward my choices.
- Strategy: I create short-term and long-term goals to propel my mission.
- Accountability: I make myself responsible to God and others for achieving my goals and mission.
- Communication: I produce a written document to embed my vision, mission, and goals in my heart, soul, and mind.

Prioritize. Jesus teaches in Matthew 6:33 that God's kingdom and His commands come first; everything else is secondary. Priorities supply direction for accomplishing God's will. Properly considered, a good plan governs my choices—yes, no, and maybe later. If I don't prioritize my daily activities, the day fritters away without anything to show for it. A good plan disciplines my use of time to make it meaningful.

Trust. I plan because I trust God. In Matthew 6:25-32, there is a list of concerns and worries, no different than worries we have today, and Jesus says that if we put Him first, *"all these things will be added to you."* Isaiah 26:3 says, *"You keep him in perfect peace whose mind is stayed on you, because he trusts in you."* A good plan relieves anxiety because it trusts in the power and provision of a God who wants me to join Him in doing His will.

In closing, theologian Dallas Willard asks, *"will we have faith to do the things that will secure us in the goodness of God, in 'his righteousness,' or will we neglect them, and lose our lives in inefficient and futile struggles with powers that are too great for us?"* We can answer affirmatively when we plan, prioritize, and trust.

— KEY VERSE —

But seek first the kingdom of God and his righteousness, and all these things will be added to you. (Matthew 6:33)

Hello mornings

God. Plan. Move.

READ : Matthew 6:25-33
WRITE : Matthew 6:33

. . . .

REFLECT :
– What are the four anxious thoughts addressed in Matthew 6:25-33? What is Jesus' response to each? How does this passage encourage you to walk in faith today?
– Locate the planning resources available through *www.hellomornings.org*. Try a freebie!
– Who or what are your priorities? Ask God if your priorities align with His purpose?
– Research the New Testament Greek meaning for the word *anxious* from today's passage.
– Entrust your anxious thoughts to God in prayer.

RESPOND :

. . . .

PLAN TIME

THINGS TO DO (3-5 MAX) :

KEY EVENTS TODAY :

MOVE TIME

MORNING WATER ☐

B : _____
L : _____
D : _____

SNACK :

SIMPLE WORKOUT ☐

WEEK 4, DAY 3: PROVERBS 3:5-6; 16:9; ISAIAH 55:8; EPHESIANS 3:20-21

I MUCK OUT HORSE STALLS as a volunteer for an equine therapy organization serving special needs students alongside my daughters. I am not a barns, shovels, and manure kind of girl, but I believe God used an unplanned, out-of-the-box opportunity to strengthen my relationship with my daughters. As I work to accomplish God's will, I make plans, but I allow God to lead. I am growing in my ability to flex, yield, and follow God's direction.

Flex. Flexing keeps me nimble, so I can adjust my plans. When I plan or establish a routine, I am prone to legalism in keeping it. On one hand, I feel good about sticking to the plan, but on the other, it fuels my pride about maintaining discipline and control. Proverbs 16:9 reminds me otherwise: *"The heart of Man plans his way, but the Lord establishes his steps."* As I work to do God's will, I must be willing to flex and adapt to a new idea, person, or opportunity God provides. It might just be the missing piece that makes a good plan a great plan.

Yield. Yielding keeps me humble. When I plan, I must be willing to give up my plans and allow God to have His way. Kat Lee says, *"Our schedules and plans should always be a sacrifice and not an idol."* Sacrifice is a complete yielding of what is ours into the hands of God. Yielding maintains a proper relationship to God; He is my master, and I am His servant. God says, *"For my thoughts are not your thoughts, neither are your ways, my ways. . ."* (Isaiah 55:8). I cannot out-think, out-give, or out-love God. I must allow His opportunities to overtake my plans.

Follow. Following keeps me in God's will. When God plots the path, I must follow wholeheartedly. Following God's path is not always easy, but it is always best. When my husband and I obeyed God and took the only job available thousands of miles away from "home," God gave us an amazing five years in a new place, with new people, leaving us forever changed. It wasn't easy, but it was best and exceeded our expectations. Ephesians 3:20 says that God *"is able to do immeasurably more than we can ask or imagine."* In order to live out God's will, I trust Him to lead the way.

So, when we plan, we plan prepared to adjust, surrender, and conform to the purpose God has ordained for us. In doing so, we fulfill His will—even in a horse stall.

— KEY VERSE —

The heart of man plans his way, but the Lord establishes his steps. (Proverbs 16:9)

Hello mornings

God. Plan. Move.

READ : Proverbs 3:5-6; 16:9; Isaiah 55:8; Ephesians 3:20-21
WRITE : Proverbs 16:9

. . . .

. . . .

REFLECT :
- Memorize a scripture included in today's reading plan.
- Assign a headline to each of the Scriptures in today's reading plan. What are these Scriptures impressing on your head and heart?
- Read Romans 11:33-36, and compare it to Isaiah 55:9. What do you learn?
- Which plans do you resist yielding to God? Confess it to Him and surrender in prayer.
- Listen to Hello Mornings Podcast, HM 35, at *www.hellomornings.org/podcast*.

RESPOND :

. . . .

. . . .

. . . .

. . . .

PLAN TIME

THINGS TO DO (3-5 MAX) :

KEY EVENTS TODAY :

MOVE TIME

MORNING WATER ☐

B : _____
L : _____
D : _____

SNACK :

SIMPLE WORKOUT ☐

WEEK 4, DAY 4: JAMES 4:13-17

IT IS ENERGIZING TO DREAM ABOUT THE FUTURE and how we can serve God, but we need to transform our plans into daily activity. God wants us to serve Him today and leave the future in His hands. Kat Lee's book, *Hello Mornings: How to Build a Grace-Filled, Life-Giving Morning Routine*, reminds me to assess, prioritize, and adjust my appointments and tasks to sync with God's purpose every day.

Assess. The New Testament writer, James says, *". . . you do not know what tomorrow will bring"* (James 4:14a). Tomorrow is not guaranteed; we must practice being present today and live it the best we can. Too many times, my day has been thrown into a tizzy because I didn't review my appointments and tasks for the day. We can't serve God well when we're frazzled—especially when we do it to ourselves. A quick minute or two is all you need to review your calendar and "to-do" list, preparing yourself to successfully accomplish the day.

Prioritize. James continues in the same passage, *". . . you are a mist that appears for a little time and then vanishes"* (James 4:14b). If our lives are a blip on the continuum of eternity, we need to prioritize our activities to make the most of the time God gives us. Stephen Covey teaches people to schedule "first things first"—important relationships, projects, and purpose-filled activities. The laundry, emails, social media, and other less important activities can fill in around your priorities. Arrange tasks in order of priority, get the important tasks done, and avoid being sabotaged by the mundane.

Adjust. Sometimes we get caught up in the everyday and forget that God is in charge. James addresses this, saying, *"Instead you ought to say, 'If the Lord wills, we will live and do this or that'"* (James 4:15). After you've reviewed your calendar and "to-do" list and arranged your tasks and appointments by priority, offer your plans to the Lord in prayer. Ask Him to show you if anything needs to be removed or added. Ask Him to guide you as you move through the day. Linger a bit in silence. Listen to God, and yield your plans to Him. Obey by making the changes to your plans that He impresses on your heart and mind.

When we take a few minutes at the start of the day to assess, prioritize, and adjust our plans, we make the most of our day and leave control where it belongs—with God.

—  —

Instead you ought to say, "If the Lord wills, we will live and do this or that." (James 4:15)

Hello mornings

God. Plan. Move.

READ : James 4:13-17
WRITE : James 4:15

....

....

REFLECT :
- Download and read the first chapter of the *Hello Mornings* book by Hello Mornings founder, Kat Lee. It's free! Here's the link: *https://www.hellomornings.org/book*.
- Write a personal paraphrase of James 4:13-17.
- Use the Plan Time section below to quickly review tasks and events today.
- Arrange your tasks according to importance.
- Offer your plans to the Lord in prayer. Spend time listening for His direction.

RESPOND :

....

....

....

....

....

....

PLAN TIME

THINGS TO DO (3-5 MAX) :

KEY EVENTS TODAY :

MOVE TIME

MORNING WATER ☐

B : _____
L : _____
D : _____

SNACK :

SIMPLE WORKOUT ☐

WEEK 4, DAY 5: JOHN 17:4; ROMANS 14:12; 1 JOHN 2:3-6

I AM CURRENTLY NAVIGATING through a season of transition. Free to explore new interests and hone new skills while I create and adjust plans, I must remain accountable to doing God's will, not my own. Throughout my life I am accountable not only to others but also to myself and God.

Others. Our plans impact our families, close friends, circles of influence, acquaintances and passers-by. When we are living out God's purpose, others see God because they see the results of a life lived for God. Jesus said to the Father, *"I glorified you on earth, having accomplished the work that you gave me to do"* (John 17:4). Jesus is our role model, and as He glorified the Father by completing His mission for the Father, we are to do the same. We can encourage accountability by asking other believers to join us—encouraging and exhorting each other along the way.

Self. God equips us with the Holy Spirit, so we know when we're right with God and when we are not. We are responsible for living in accordance with God's will: *"Whoever says 'I know him' but does not keep his commandments is a liar, and the truth is not in him. . ."* (1 John 2:4). This verse speaks to our personal integrity; we can't say one thing and do another. In the next verse we read, *". . . By this we may know that we are in him: whoever says he abides in him ought to walk in the same way in which he walked."* (1 John 2:5b-6). As Jesus carried out God's will with excellence, I am called to do the same. However, God doesn't ask for my perfection; He asks for my best. God supplies ample grace for my shortcomings and makes perfect what I cannot.

God. Of course, we're accountable to God. We can't escape it: *"So then each of us will give an account of himself to God"* (Romans 14:12). As part of His creation, God expects us to steward our relationships, time, and purpose to be effective in our service to Him. Stewardship doesn't happen haphazardly; it occurs with intention, thought and planning. When we stand before God, our deeds and accomplishments will bear witness to our faithfulness to God's will.

No matter what season you're in, join me in deciding today to plan for God's purpose. May this prayer from Psalm 143:10 be ours, *"Teach me to do your will, for you are my God! Let your good Spirit lead me on level ground!"*

—  —

So then each of us will give an account of himself to God. (Romans 14:12)

Hello mornings

God. Plan. Move.

READ : John 17:4; Romans 14:12; 1 John 2:3-6
WRITE : Romans 14:12

....

....

REFLECT :
- Journal about a time when you experienced God's pleasure for doing His will.
- Contrast your impact on the people around you when you're living out God's will and when you fail to live out His will.
- What does it mean to *"walk in the same way in which he [Jesus] walked"* (1 John 2:6)?
- Ask the Holy Spirit to show you where your life and God's purpose aren't in sync.
- Going forward, how will you steward your relationships, time, and purpose for God?

RESPOND :

....

....

....

....

....

PLAN TIME

THINGS TO DO (3-5 MAX) :

MOVE TIME

MORNING WATER ☐

B : _____

L : _____

D : _____

KEY EVENTS TODAY :

SNACK :

SIMPLE WORKOUT ☐

WEEK 5, DAY 1: 1 CORINTHIANS 6:19-20

ONE OF THE MOST COMMON WORDS for toddlers is the word "mine." Maybe you've seen this in your own child or a child you know. What's theirs is theirs, and what's yours is theirs as soon as they want it. Sharing is hard for kids!

In reality, though, sharing isn't only difficult for children. It's also hard for adults. We all struggle to think of something that is "ours" being someone else's. We want our money to be ours, our bodies to be ours, and our stuff to be ours.

What 1 Corinthians 6:19-20 tells us, however, is that we're not our own. *"You are not your own,"* it says, *"for you were bought with a price."* That price was the life of Jesus. He paid for us with His own blood shed on the cross.

The language here reminds us of a slave auction. Just as a slave is no longer free to do as they wish, so also we who have given our lives to Jesus cannot continue to do whatever we want. That might sound like slavery, and it should since that is the language Paul uses. In reality, though, when we do whatever we want, we become enslaved to sin.

What it comes down to is this: we can be enslaved to sin, or we can be enslaved to Jesus. Those are our only options. I don't know about you, but I'd much rather be enslaved to Jesus, who only wants what is best for me and who is working all things out for my good.

What it means for us to be enslaved to Jesus is that we don't live for ourselves alone. Our time isn't ours to do with as we please. Our bodies aren't ours. Neither is our stuff, our thoughts, or our money. Each of us has been bought with a price, so now, we no longer live for ourselves.

Rather, we live for Jesus, and we seek to glorify Him in everything we do and say. This week, as you go about your day, remember that you are not your own. When you accepted Jesus as your Savior, you also accepted Him as your Lord. You can't have one without the other.

— KEY VERSE —

Or do you not know that your body is a temple of the Holy Spirit within you, whom you have from God? You are not your own, for you were bought with a price. So glorify God in your body. (1 Corinthians 6:19-20)

Hello mornings

God. Plan. Move.

READ : 1 Corinthians 6:19-20
WRITE : 1 Corinthians 6:19-20

REFLECT :
- Write out 1 Corinthians 6:19-20 in your own words.
- Research the Corinthian church. What was going on there when Paul wrote this letter?
- How does the context of today's text help you understand Paul's original meaning?
- Read Romans 6:20-23. What does it mean to be a slave to Christ?
- What do you think hinders most Christians from giving everything to God? Is there anything in your life that you haven't fully given to God? If so, what?

RESPOND :

PLAN TIME

THINGS TO DO (3-5 MAX) :

KEY EVENTS TODAY :

MOVE TIME

MORNING WATER ☐

B : _____
L : _____
D : _____

SNACK :

SIMPLE WORKOUT ☐

WEEK 5, DAY 2: 1 CORINTHIANS 10:24, 31-33; 11:1

HAVE YOU EVER SEEN A BODY OF STAGNANT WATER? It can look pretty disgusting, can't it? It can also be very dangerous. Stagnant water can become a breeding ground for mosquitoes and can cause deadly diseases in humans. Water, by God's design, isn't supposed to just sit there, unmoving. It's designed to flow.

In a similar way, when God pours Himself and His Word and His Spirit into us, He intends for us to pour into others. We aren't supposed to be stagnant, simply taking in and taking in and never pouring out.

Imagine a pitcher full of lemonade. As the lemonade is poured into a glass, the glass fills to the brim with delicious beverage. Then, as the pitcher keeps flowing, the lemonade spills over the edges of the cup and onto everything around it. That's how we are supposed to be with our faith.

God pours Himself into us, and we overflow His Spirit into the lives of those around us. When we fail to do this, we can become stagnant. When we let God fill us up but then refuse to overflow into others through service, acts of kindness, and love, we turn into disease-ridden water.

This week, as you think about God's call for your life and your response to that call, don't forget about your fellow brothers and sisters in Christ. God doesn't call us to something purely for our benefit. Rather, He calls us to something so that we can benefit others.

Paul says in 1 Corinthians 10:24, "Let no one seek his own good, but the good of his neighbor." In context, Paul said this because there were questions about eating food sacrificed to idols. Paul was saying that though we have freedom in Christ, we should not use this freedom to hurt someone else. We should always—in everything we do—not only think about ourselves but also think about how our actions affect those around us.

God's game plan is like this: He pours into us. We pour into others. Then they, in turn, will pour into those around them, and the cycle will continue as God designed it.

This week, how can you seek the good of those around you? How can you seek the good of your spouse? Your children? How can you seek the good of your co-workers? What can you do or say this week that will show them Jesus.

—  KEY VERSE —

Let no one seek his own good, but the good of his neighbor. (1 Corinthians 10:24)

Hello mornings

God. Plan. Move.

READ : 1 Corinthians 10:24, 31-33; 11:1
WRITE : 1 Corinthians 10:24

. . . .

. . . .

REFLECT :
- Write out 1 Corinthians 11:1. What are some characteristics of Jesus you want to imitate?
- What are some practical ways you can pour God's Spirit on to those around you?
- Why is it sometimes difficult to seek the good of our neighbors?
- What do today's verses tell us about God?
- What do today's verses tell us about ourselves?

RESPOND :

. . . .

. . . .

. . . .

. . . .

PLAN TIME

THINGS TO DO (3-5 MAX) :

KEY EVENTS TODAY :

MOVE TIME

MORNING WATER ☐

B : _____

L : _____

D : _____

SNACK :

SIMPLE WORKOUT ☐

WEEK 5, DAY 3: ISAIAH 6:8; HEBREWS 12:1

A FEW WEEKS AGO, I attended a retreat designed to help deepen my faith in Jesus. At that retreat, one of the speakers shared about common roadblocks to following God's call in our lives. One of those roadblocks was other Christians.

Specifically, the speaker mentioned Christian parents discouraging their kids from following God's call. These parents love Jesus. They want to follow Him. But they also want easy, safe lives for their kids. They don't want their kids to follow God's call, if God's call means moving far away or going somewhere that's unsafe.

The truth is, God never promised us His call would be easy. He never promised us His call would keep us safe in the way we typically think of safety. What He did promise us is that His call would be good. His call would bring us joy. His call would lead us into greater freedom than we ever thought possible.

In Isaiah 6:8, when Isaiah heard the Lord asking who He could send, Isaiah cried out, *"Here I am! Send me."* He was willing—eager even—to go where the Lord wanted him to go. I wonder, are we as willing and eager to do what God has called us to do?

Maybe, as you're reading through this study, you're not even sure what God's call is for you. You're willing but have no idea what He wants. If this is you, there are two places to look.

The first place is in God's Word. If you want to know what God wants for you, there is no better place to start than the Bible.

In it, we learn God wants us to love Him, first and foremost, and to love our neighbors as ourselves (Matthew 22:34-40). In it, we learn God wants us to act justly, to love mercy, and to be humble (Micah 6:8). In it, we learn God wants us to set our minds on things above (Colossians 3:2). Much of God's call for His followers can be found on the pages of His Word.

If you're not sure what God's call is for you, look to the Word first. Start there. Then, after exploring the Bible, look at your gifts and abilities. How has God gifted you, and how can you use these talents for His glory and for the encouragement of those around you.

— KEY VERSE —

And I heard the voice of the Lord saying, "Whom shall I send, and who will go for us?" Then I said, "Here I am! Send me." (Isaiah 6:8)

Hello mornings

God. Plan. Move.

GOD TIME

READ : Isaiah 6:8; Hebrews 12:1
WRITE : Isaiah 6:8

....

....

REFLECT :
- Read Hebrews 12:1. What hinders you from following God's call?
- Based on Scriptures you've read before, make a list of some of the things that you know God wants from you.
- What gifts and abilities has God given you? List them.
- How might God want to use these gifts for His glory?
- What is the primary take-away from Isaiah 6:8.

RESPOND :

....

....

....

....

....

PLAN TIME

THINGS TO DO (3-5 MAX) :

KEY EVENTS TODAY :

MOVE TIME

MORNING WATER ☐

B : _____

L : _____

D : _____

SNACK :

SIMPLE WORKOUT ☐

WEEK 5, DAY 4: ROMANS 12:1-8

WHEN WE THINK OF SACRIFICE, we think of giving something up for someone. For instance, I sacrifice sleep when my kids are sick. We might also sacrifice money, time, or that last piece of cheesecake for someone we love.

Many of us, when we hear the word *sacrifice*, think of brave military men and women who have sacrificed their lives for our freedom. We might also think of police officers or firefighters or other emergency workers who sacrifice their lives to help others.

Our picture of a sacrifice is different than what Old Testament Israelites likely pictured. For them, when someone said *sacrifice*, they likely pictured the altar that animals were offered on or maybe the animals themselves.

Though the pictures are different, the ideas behind them are the same. A sacrifice is something that is given up. In Romans 12:1, Paul commanded the Christians in Rome to present their *"bodies as a living sacrifice, holy and acceptable to God."* This, he said, is an act of worship.

So, if a sacrifice is something that is given up, what does it mean to offer yourself as a living sacrifice? It means you give up your rights. It means you let God take the reins in your life. As you are living, you are not living for yourself but for God. In essence, it means that Jesus is in charge of you. He's in charge of what you say, what you do, how you spend your money, how you dress, what you think, and how you live your life each day.

One other important aspect of being a living sacrifice is that it's a daily thing. You can't just sacrifice one time and call it good. It's something you have to do over and over again.

I don't know about you, but giving up my desires is difficult! Deep down, I'm selfish, and I want what I want. Being a living sacrifice means I try my best to give that up each and every day.

There's a common saying that the problem with a living sacrifice is that it keeps crawling off the altar. I'm not sure who originally said this, but it's a great quote, isn't it? This week, don't let that be true of you. Stay on that altar."

— KEY VERSE —

I appeal to you therefore, brothers, by the mercies of God, to present your bodies as a living sacrifice, holy and acceptable to God, which is your spiritual worship. (Romans 12:1)

Hello mornings

God. Plan. Move.

READ : Romans 12:1-8
WRITE : Romans 12:1

....

....

REFLECT :
- Why is it difficult to be a "living sacrifice" to God?
- Research the Old Testament sacrificial system to gain a deeper understanding of what it means to offer a sacrifice.
- Is there anything in your life that you are not yet willing to give up to God? Pray about this.
- What in your life needs to change as a result of today's Scripture?
- Underline the words *living sacrifice* in your Bible.

RESPOND :

....

....

....

....

....

PLAN TIME

THINGS TO DO (3-5 MAX) :

MOVE TIME

MORNING WATER ☐

B : _____

L : _____

D : _____

KEY EVENTS TODAY :

SNACK :

SIMPLE WORKOUT ☐

WEEK 5, DAY 5: 1 CORINTHIANS 9:24-27

A FEW YEARS AGO, I decided I wanted to run a half-marathon. Now, before you start thinking I'm one of those people who actually enjoys running, there's something you should know about me: I'm not really a runner. I run occasionally, but it's more because I need to than because I want to.

Eric Liddell, a Christian man and also an Olympic athlete, said that when he ran, he felt God's pleasure. As much as I would like to say the same for myself, that's not the case. When I run, I feel out of shape, tired, and tempted to quit. Nonetheless, because I got it in my head that I needed to do a half-marathon, I trained. I trained and I trained and I trained.

I did that because I wanted to reach my goal, and my goal was to complete the race without stopping. In 1 Corinthians 9:25, Paul told the Corinthians, *"Everyone who competes in the games goes into strict training. They do it to get a crown that will not last, but we do it to get a crown that will last forever"* (NIV). When I trained for that race, I pushed myself, and it was worth it because it worked. I reached my goal.

Unfortunately, the sad reality about running is that you lose your progress quickly if you stop running. As soon as the race was over, I stopped training and quickly lost the ability to run long distances. That's because I was training for something that didn't last.

On the other hand, when we train for spiritual things, we train for things that last for eternity. That's why spiritual disciplines are so important: they outlast us.

Maybe you're reading this and are unsure what a spiritual discipline even is, let alone how to begin incorporating one into your life. If this is you, here is an easy definition. A spiritual discipline is a practice that helps develop your faith. It's a habit that, when done regularly, builds your spiritual life.

Some spiritual disciplines include: Bible study, Bible memorization, prayer, fasting, worship, meditation, and service. When we do these things, we train for something that matters for eternity. We train for heaven.

— KEY VERSE —

Do you not know that in a race all the runners run, but only one gets the prize? Run in such a way as to get the prize. Everyone who competes in the games goes into strict training. They do it to get a crown that will not last, but we do it to get a crown that will last forever. (1 Corinthians 9:24-25, NIV)

Hello mornings

God. Plan. Move.

READ : 1 Corinthians 9:24-27
WRITE : 1 Corinthians 9:24-25

REFLECT :
- Read 1 Timothy 4:8. How does this verse relate to today's text?
- Memorize 1 Timothy 4:8.
- Check out the book, *Spiritual Disciplines for the Christian Life*, by Donald S. Whitney. Consider reading this book as part of your spiritual training.
- Which spiritual discipline would you like to begin incorporating into your life first?
- What is your greatest obstacle to making spiritual disciplines a regular part of your life?

RESPOND :

PLAN TIME

THINGS TO DO (3-5 MAX) :

KEY EVENTS TODAY :

MOVE TIME

MORNING WATER ☐

B : _____
L : _____
D : _____

SNACK :

SIMPLE WORKOUT ☐

WEEK 6, DAY 1: 1 CORINTHIANS 10:13; ROMANS 8:31, 37; 1 JOHN 5:1-5

WHEN I WAS VERY SMALL, my mother bought latch hook kits for my older siblings and me. One day, while working hard making my little square of carpet, my mother peeked in my room, saw me bent over my work, and laughed. In a confused voice, I asked what was funny. Her response? "Well, I've never seen anyone use *their feet* when they worked a latch hook rug!" To me, it just made sense to steady the work with my toes. My fingers were then free to do the hard job of looping yarn over the hook and pulling it through the canvas grid.

The verses we're reading today may not initially seem to go together with the "Move" portion of our study. Yet, all of today's verses tell us about temptations and the power to overcome them. When we set goals of health for ourselves, we need to be aware that temptations will come to distract us and get in our way. We need to know where to access power to overcome them!

As we've discussed in this study, God has a plan for each of us. As we connect with Him each morning and plan our days to include His will, it also follows that we need to care for our bodies in a way that gives us the energy and endurance to fulfill His call.

Part of taking care of ourselves to walk out His calling includes saying no to certain things. As we learn to say "no" to things that are not healthy nor wise and ask for His strength in doing so, we free up time and energy that can instead be placed in saying "yes" to what God has asked.

Like what is written in 1 John 5:1-5, God's commands are not burdensome. Neither is His plan for us. When we work in conjunction with the power of the Holy Spirit, He equips us (Hebrews 13:20-21) and renews us (2 Corinthians 4:16) in our Christian walk. On our own strength, we may not have the power to resist temptations or help ourselves, but by partnering with His mighty resurrection power in us (see Ephesians 1:19-23), we can!

What is God calling you to do today? What needs to go in order to strengthen your body to apply your heart for God's service? When you say no to temptations that distract you from your calling, it's a bit like using your feet to make a latch hook rug. Now your hands are free to do God's work.

— KEY VERSE —

No temptation has overtaken you that is not common to man. God is faithful, and he will not let you be tempted beyond your ability, but with the temptation he will also provide the way of escape, that you may be able to endure it. (1 Corinthians 10:13)

Hello mornings

God. Plan. Move.

READ : 1 Corinthians 10:13; Romans 8:31, 37; 1 John 5:1-5
WRITE : 1 Corinthians 10:13

. . . .

. . . .

REFLECT :
- We read from three passages today. Which one stands out most to you and why?
- Research how Jesus responded to Satan's temptations. Let that be your model.
- Read Romans 8:31-39. How does this expound on God's strength?
- How does knowing God's strength encourage you to fight against temptations?
- What is God calling you to do? Write down what you can say "no" to today to help "free your hands" to work that calling.

RESPOND :

. . . .

. . . .

. . . .

. . . .

PLAN TIME

THINGS TO DO (3-5 MAX) :

KEY EVENTS TODAY :

MOVE TIME

MORNING WATER ☐

B : _____

L : _____

D : _____

SNACK :

SIMPLE WORKOUT ☐

WEEK 6, DAY 2: MATTHEW 9:35-38

ON A REGULAR BASIS, my husband sets aside time to thoroughly check our vehicle. He believes that regular maintenance is critical for the longevity of our cars and for the safety of our family. Periodically, he'll measure and top off all fluid levels, check the tire pressure and various gauges, and tinker with things I can't even name. The point? He wants to be a good steward of what God has given and make sure that we are properly equipped for safe travels.

In today's passage we read about Jesus travelling throughout *"all the cities and villages,"* teaching the Gospel. (Matthew 9:35) This particular event was fairly early in His ministry. Jesus saw the people's need and was motivated by compassion. He then spread the doctrine of salvation among the shepherdless people, calling them into His fold. But to accomplish this work, He had to go and do.

In order to accomplish God's will in our lives, we must give our faith "feet," so that we, too, can go and do. Caring for our physical needs readies us to answer His spiritual call. When our mind, body, and emotions are at their healthiest, we won't tire as easily when keeping up with our children, helping our husbands, serving in our churches, or praying in earnest for others. Whether it's going on a run, doing a short wake-up workout, or simply drinking a glass of water, making a healthy choice each morning is a great way to start and stay a good steward of ourselves! It takes energy and endurance to continually say yes to God.

A couple of years ago, I injured my knee badly and many of my health goals and routines had to change. There's a lot I'm still not sure of. But what I do know is this: I can do what I can do and if I don't take care of myself, I won't even be able to do that. Sisters, not all of us are strong, healthy athletes, and Jesus doesn't ask us to be. But He does want us to present our bodies as a living sacrifice to Him (Romans 12:1). If we are in a season where we can "only" use our bodies to pray for other laborers to be sent to the harvest, dear friend, that is enough!

We are all laborers, sent to do His will. Meeting with Him each morning and choosing to steward our bodies *well* prepares and equips us to go and do His good work of Gospel-living and Gospel-sharing.

— KEY VERSE —

Therefore pray earnestly to the Lord of the harvest to send out laborers into his harvest. (Matthew 9:38)

Hello mornings

God. Plan. Move.

READ : Matthew 9:35-38
WRITE : Matthew 9:38

....

....

REFLECT :
– Today's passage has a lot of action words. Take note of them. What do you learn?
– Use the passage: Who are the laborers? Why are they needed?
– Research the spiritual harvest: *https://www.gotquestions.org/spiritual-harvest.html*
– What season are you in? Know that whatever season, God can use you! Pray for Him to send you, or to send others to work His harvest.
– Ask God to help you manage your energy so you can "go and do" His purposes.

RESPOND :

....

....

....

....

PLAN TIME

THINGS TO DO (3-5 MAX) :

KEY EVENTS TODAY :

MOVE TIME

MORNING WATER ☐

B : _____
L : _____
D : _____

SNACK :

SIMPLE WORKOUT ☐

"HE SAYS HE CAN'T DO ANYTHING BUT LAY AND PRAY." My sweet cousin-by-marriage shared the story of her precious grandfather with me. At that time, the World War II veteran who'd once been strong and vigorous, now lay in bed dying. Instead of feeling sorry for himself, this faithful man of God was hungry to pray for others. So, lay and pray he did! Up until his last breath, he was obediently giving what he could to honor the Lord.

In Mark 14:3-9 we read of a woman applauded by Jesus. While Christ was in Bethany visiting at Simon the Leper's home, Mary of Bethany*, of Mary and Martha fame (see John 12:3 and Luke 10:38-42), came to anoint the Savior in preparation for His burial.

Mary was evidently well off and her gift expensive, so I find it interesting that Jesus used the words, *"she has done what she could."* Since acts of honoring God are about the heart and not about the monetary value, Jesus didn't say, *"Wow, she's done so much because of the money she spent on me!"* Instead, he says, *"she has done what she could."* To me, Jesus implies she acted from the heart and it was enough. When we do all we can do, it will be enough, too.

In Luke 21:1-4 we see this principle described further. In the temple courts, chests were set up for the Jews to drop in their offerings. A poor widow came along and dropped in about $2.00. Like Mary of Bethany, she did what she could. The widow's offering was small in earthly comparison, but Jesus didn't think so! Jesus commended her generosity and said that she had given more than all the rest. Like my friend's grandfather, she gave all she could!

So what does all of this have to do with the "Move" theme of Hello Mornings? Let's back up to something I said yesterday. God wants *"us to present our bodies as a living sacrifice to Him"* (Romans 12:1). We may feel our current season is full of "small offerings." But even if we can "only" pray for other laborers to be sent, it's enough! Each morning, we have the choice to give God our all, understanding that it will look different from person to person. We can daily make wise choices so that our bodies can be a healthy temple for God's Spirit in us. Presenting our bodies to Him is a way we can honor Jesus with all we have.

— KEY VERSE —

And he said, "Truly, I tell you, this poor widow has put in more than all of them." (Luke 21:3)

*Though Mary of Bethany is unnamed in today's Bible reading, most scholars agree to her identity because she is named in the parallel passage in John 12:1-8.

Hello mornings

God. Plan. Move.

READ : Mark 14:3-9; Luke 21:1-4
WRITE : Luke 21:3

. . . .

. . . .

REFLECT :

– Outline the passages. Think about what Jesus is saying. What stands out to you?
– Read Mark 14:4 and John 12:4-6. Judas was selfish. Contrast him with Mary of Bethany.
  How can taking care of God's temple (our bodies) be unselfish?
– Read Romans 12:1 and 1 Corinthians 6:19-20 and 10:31. What is God saying?
– Pray that God will help you not compare your healthy choices with someone else's.
– Ask Jesus to help you give Him your best, then share today's message with a friend.

RESPOND :

. . . .

. . . .

. . . .

. . . .

. . . .

PLAN TIME

THINGS TO DO (3-5 MAX) :

KEY EVENTS TODAY :

MOVE TIME

MORNING WATER ☐

B : _____

L : _____

D : _____

SNACK :

SIMPLE WORKOUT ☐

WEEK 6, DAY 4: JOHN 13:1-11

HER BARE FEET HAD GOTTEN DIRTY PLAYING OUTSIDE, so when my neighbor's child came in the house I lifted her onto the bathroom counter and washed her feet in the sink. She sweetly said, "Oh, Mrs. Ali, I'm sorry you have to do this for me." I laughed and told her that I really liked serving my friends. I got to tell her about how Jesus took care of His friends, too, and even washed their feet. She was amazed! But the coolest thing? This unusual opportunity that God surprised me with just happened to arise on Maundy Thursday, the very day that Christians commemorate Jesus' acts in today's passage!

Sisters, we are called to wash one another's feet. We are called to serve, to give, to love, to be the body of Christ, to share the Gospel, and do other "greater works." (See John 14:12) But how do we do it? It usually involves some elbow grease and lots of prayer. As Jesus is a servant, so we should be.

Jesus teaches us that when it comes time to serve, we really should just get busy doing it. Notice that John 13:2 says, "During supper" Jesus had a realization and then (in verse four) He "rose from supper." Once He knew what He should do, He did it, even though it was what we might call a "surprise opportunity" that interrupted His meal. He jumped right into the nitty-gritty of serving with humility, looking to the interests of others (Philippians 2:4).

In Kat Lee's book, Hello Mornings: How to Build a Grace-Filled, Life-Giving Morning Routine, she says, "Our health affects more than just how we look. It affects how we feel, how we act, the decisions we make, and our ability to focus and succeed at the opportunities God has given us. ...Let's focus on building our energy to serve rather than building our image to impress."

Kat's last sentence looks an awful lot like Jesus in action, doesn't it? Stripped for work, down on the floor, washing dirty feet, He reminds us that service certainly isn't about impressing others. Instead, service is about the other person's greater good. It isn't usually easy for the one doing the work, but by making healthy choices, we are better fit to serve like Him and get busy making use of those surprise opportunities God gives us.

— KEY VERSE —

[Jesus] rose from supper. He laid aside his outer garments, and taking a towel, tied it around his waist. Then he poured water into a basin and began to wash the disciples' feet...(John 13:4-5a)

Hello mornings

God. Plan. Move.

READ : John 13:1-11
WRITE : John 13:4-5a

. . . .

. . . .

REFLECT :
- What stands out to you most in today's passage? Why?
- Research the Biblical account of foot washing. What did you learn about service?
- See 1 Peter 4:10-11, Acts 20:35, and Mark 10:45. Write down what is said about serving.
- Move time is about energy for God's call, not image. How does that perspective free you?
- Prayerfully examine your days and ask God to help you be physically ready for any surprise opportunities He may send.

RESPOND :

. . . .

. . . .

. . . .

. . . .

. . . .

PLAN TIME

THINGS TO DO (3-5 MAX) :

KEY EVENTS TODAY :

MOVE TIME

MORNING WATER ☐

B : _____
L : _____
D : _____

SNACK :

SIMPLE WORKOUT ☐

MY FRIEND RECENTLY WENT ON A SERVICE TRIP. Helping others looked like handing out food, cleaning tables, lifting and carrying heavy bags, and being on her feet almost all day. As she jokingly shared on social media, "Twelve hour days are tough on the old lady!" The gentleman with limited mobility who was assigned with her gave a different type of service. Because he had differing abilities, God didn't call him to do the same things that my friend did. But in both cases, I can guarantee, service was tiring and caring for their bodies was crucial.

In today's passage, Jesus explains the foot washing we read about yesterday. Christ tells the disciples that He is willing to occupy a low place of servanthood. He tells them that if they want to be like Him, their Lord and Teacher, they should serve as He did. Jesus shows us that service often looks like sitting on the floor with a dirty foot in the face.

What low place of servanthood do you occupy? Are you like my friend, handing out food and wiping tables? Or are you wiping noses, changing diapers (baby or adult ones), and feeding mouths? If you're in a season of relentless work, you know well that we can all get tired from serving! (Friend, I had a rough moment earlier today, when I felt so tired I almost said things I'd really regret.) So, where do we get the physical energy we've been talking about the past few days? How can we keep going with gentleness, kindness, and the compassion of Christ?

The physical energy to serve comes from three very practical sources: sleep, hydration, and nutrition. Once those basics are provided, exercise can then be added for a boost in strength and endurance. As we read and study Jesus' example, we realize we need to treat our bodies practically as well as spiritually. Our spiritual act of worship is giving Him our bodies. In practical terms, that is done by caring for our bodies.

Our practical choices affect our spiritual ones. If we do not care for our bodies, we won't be able to serve the Lord with joy and love like Jesus did. God. Plan. Move. It makes a full circle, doesn't it? We seek to follow the Lord and His will, then pray to include time in our days to carry out His call, and care for ourselves in a way that enables us to serve with a Jesus-filled heart. All for His glory.

— KEY VERSE —

For I have given you an example, that you also should do just as I have done to you. (John 13:15)

Hello mornings

God. Plan. Move.

READ : John 13:12-20
WRITE : John 13:15

....

....

REFLECT :
- Outline what Jesus tells us in this passage.
- What truths, promises, and commands do you see here?
- What do these verses say about *doing*? John 13:17, Hebrews 12:1, and Luke 11:28.
- What do you think about the circle of "God. Plan. Move?" How does each core component relate? How can they all be spiritual? In what ways are they practical?
- Ask God for a strong spiritual foundation to support the physical act of serving.

RESPOND :

....

....

....

....

PLAN TIME

THINGS TO DO (3-5 MAX) :

KEY EVENTS TODAY :

MOVE TIME

MORNING WATER ☐

B : _____
L : _____
D : _____

SNACK :

SIMPLE WORKOUT ☐

CONCLUSION

DID YOU ENJOY OUR EXPLORATION? We dove into God's Word to see what He says about the importance of time with Him and why we seek Him. We also looked at what the Bible has to say about planning and making healthy choices. Did you expect to find so much?

I love how Kat Lee likens **God. Plan. Move.** to a motorcycle, like we discussed in the introduction to this study. God is indeed our "engine" that empowers us to "go," planning is the "handlebars" that steer our days, and moving toward healthy choices is the "wheels" that keep our bodies healthy enough to travel along His road for us.

I pray that as you close this study and go on your way, you'd have a deeper understanding of the core components of Hello Mornings. I pray that God spoke to you through His Word and that He will continue to do so for your benefit and His glory!

May you continue to seek Him, plan your days around His calling, and move toward healthy choices so your body can walk His path.

In Him,

Ali

ABOUT THE AUTHORS

ALI SHAW can't believe how blessed life is! As a Central Texas wife, momma, and new grandma, Ali leads a full, grace-filled life. She serves as the HelloMornings Bible Study Director and owns and writes for *DoNotDepart.com...* and is generally in awe that God will use a regular girl like her! Woven with practical insight, her writing encourages women to seek God daily through the reading and study of His Word. Most of her writing can be found through HelloMornings or DoNotDepart, but she blogs occasionally at her personal blog, *HeartfeltReflections.wordpress.com* where

she's written an online Bible study, *Learning from Job*. She has also authored an in depth Bible study of Abigail. For information or encouragement, you can connect with her on Facebook at *www.facebook.com/heartfeltreflectionsblog*.

CHELI SIGLER lives life and pursues her God-given purpose of teaching from her home base in sunny Orlando, FL. Cheli and Matt, her husband of 20+ years, are blessed with two teenage daughters. She has experience as a professional educator and as children's ministry team leader, trainer and writer. Currently, Cheli equips missionary kids for the mission field as a volunteer at Wycliffe Bible Translators, teaches a third grade Sunday School class, is a contributing writer for DoNotDepart.com and participates in Hello Mornings as a group leader, mentor, and writer. Inviting people to sharpen their minds and soften their hearts for God's purpose and the world, Cheli shares ideas and resources on her blog, Sharpen to Soften (*https://chelisigler. wordpress.com*). Connect with Cheli on Twitter (*https://twitter.com/chelisigler*) or on Instagram (*https://www.instagram.com/chelidee/*).

KAREN BOZEMAN is a wife and empty-nester. Her adult children moved far from their East Texas roots, so she travels often. She taught high school and college for over 25 years, but is now officially retired. It is her joy to write and edit projects for her church and various ministries. Karen has been a group leader for HelloMornings for over three years and is excited to have contributed to her fifth HM project. Karen serves as the Ministry Coordinator for the thriving Connect Group that her husband teaches in their local church. In addition, Karen leads studies at several

women's shelters as well as organizing and participating in projects that benefit these women. Most often, you can find her huddled in the corner with her sewing machine, trying out the latest quilting pattern she's found on Pinterest. She and her husband have been married 40 years and enjoy traveling the globe. She would love to connect with you on Facebook at *https://www.facebook.com/kbozeman.*

LINDSEY BELL is passionate about her two silly boys and her husband Keith. She's an avid reader and a lover of all things chocolate. Lindsey is the author of the Bible study and devotional, Unbeaten, and of the parenting devotional, Searching for Sanity. She has written for several Hello Mornings studies and writes regularly for various magazines. She loves sharing with others about faith, family, and learning to love the life she's been given. As a woman who has lost four babies to miscarriage, Lindsey loves helping women find God in the midst of heartache. She would love to connect with you through her website *www.lindseymbell.com*, on Facebook, *www.facebook.com/AuthorLindseyBell*, or on Pinterest, *www.pinterest.com/LindseyMBell01.*

SABRINA GOGERTY lives with her husband and three children–two rambunctious boys and an inquisitive daughter, all seven and under–in central Iowa. She is a farm wife who happens to live in town, with a love for baking, reading, coffee, and connecting with and encouraging others. Between home life, local church ministry, and leadership in Bible Study Fellowship and Mothers of Preschoolers, there's not much time for writing these days. But whether it's putting together something for an online group of women or studying through passages for

HelloMornings, God has always seen fit to bless her heart through the discipline and joy of writing. Sabrina has found that time spent in His Word is never wasted and has joyfully been a part of HelloMornings since April of 2015.

Manufactured by Amazon.ca
Bolton, ON